T0168683

# INSTRUMENTS OF THE TRUE MEASURE

Volume 83
## Sun Tracks
*An American Indian Literary Series*

SERIES EDITOR

Ofelia Zepeda

EDITORIAL COMMITTEE

Larry Evers

Joy Harjo

Geary Hobson

N. Scott Momaday

Irvin Morris

Simon J. Ortiz

Craig Santos Perez

Kate Shanley

Leslie Marmon Silko

Luci Tapahonso

# INSTRUMENTS OF THE TRUE MEASURE

◇ POEMS ◇

LAURA DA'

THE UNIVERSITY OF
ARIZONA PRESS

TUCSON

The University of Arizona Press
www.uapress.arizona.edu

© 2018 by Laura Da'
All rights reserved. Published 2018

ISBN-13: 978-0-8165-3827-0 (paper)

Cover design by Leigh McDonald
Cover art: *Juniper Terraced Sun Shower* by Jarrod Da'

Publication of this book is made possible in part by the proceeds of a permanent endowment created with the assistance of a Challenge Grant from the National Endowment for the Humanities, a federal agency.

Library of Congress Cataloging-in-Publication Data
Names: Da', Laura, author.
Title: Instruments of the true measure : poems / Laura Da'.
Other titles: Sun tracks ; v. 83.
Description: Tucson : The University of Arizona Press, 2018. | Series: Sun tracks : an American Indian literary series ; v. 83
Identifiers: LCCN 2017056371 | ISBN 9780816538270 (pbk. : alk. paper)
Subjects: LCSH: Shawnee Indians—Poetry. | LCGFT: Poetry.
Classification: LCC PS3604.A16 I57 2018 | DDC 811/.6—dc23 LC record available at https://lccn.loc.gov/2017056371

Printed in the United States of America
♾ This paper meets the requirements of ANSI/NISO Z39.48-1992 (Permanence of Paper).

# CONTENTS

# ACKNOWLEDGMENTS

Poems from this collection have appeared in the following publications:

*Blackbird:* "Curving of the Corn," "Athwominie" (here titled "Long Hunt"), "Frontier Arithmetic," "Auction of the Bonded." *Burnside Review:* "Eating the Turtle." *Eleven Eleven:* "Mapsick," "Correction Lines," "Compass Rose." *First American Art Magazine:* "The Point of Beginnings," "Metes and Bounds," "Chains and Links." *Jack Straw Anthology:* "Instruments of the True Measure," "The Duck's Egg," "Blazed Trunk." *Lit Hub:* "First Born," "Onion Skin." *Mirrored Voices Anthology:* "Correction Lines," "Auction of the Bonded," "Allotment Line," "Axe Man," "Chains and Links." *Narrative Witness:* "Nationhood," "Timber Scribe," "Eating the Turtle," "Treaty" (here titled "The Coming Men"), "The Immaculate Grid." *The Rumpus:* "Pain Scale Treaties." *Poem of the Day, Poets.org:* "Leviathan." *Poetry Northwest:* "Compromised," "Mississippi Panorama," "The Land Crow," "The Immaculate Grid." *Toe Good:* "First Ranges." *Waxwing:* "Red Brush Surveyor," "Land Colic." *Yellow Medicine Review:* "Claws in the Water," "Obligate," "Fording," "Allotment Line."

Support from Richard Hugo House, Jack Straw Writers Program, and the Native Arts and Cultures Foundation allowed me to create this book. My deepest thanks go out to my family, friends, tribe, colleagues, students, and medical team. All the people who kept me alive and inspired for these past three years own a piece of this book and my eternal gratitude.

# INSTRUMENTS OF THE TRUE MEASURE

# NATIONHOOD

I am a citizen of two nations: Shawnee and American. I have one son who is a citizen of three. Before he was born, I learned that, like all infants, he would need to experience a change of heart at birth in order to survive. When a baby successfully breathes in through the lungs, the heart changes from parallel flow to serial flow and the shunt between the right and left atriums closes. Our new bodies obliterate old frontiers.

North America is mistakenly called nascent. The Shawnee nation is mistakenly called moribund. America established a mathematical beginning point in 1785 in what was then called the Northwest Territory. Before that, it was known in many languages as the eastern range of the Shawnee, Miami, and Huron homelands. I do not have the Shawnee words to describe this place; the notation that is available to me is 40°38′32.61″ N 80°31′9.76″ W.

# THE POINT OF BEGINNINGS

*Geodaesia: The art of surveying and measuring—*
footpath stamped and deer path trampled.

Wily agents of creation
foliated under great pressure;

white-banded rock embedded
in absolute time's alluvial fan.

The first creeping
act of range

is the infant's change of heart
from open to closed

upon the initial intake of breath.
*Thence with the meanders of the river.*

# CURVING OF THE CORN

*Crescent, b. 1812*

New Madrid earthquake quickens
      his mama's pangs.

The baby's uncle proclaims the tremor
the work of a Shawnee's
flat-footed stomp;
the father names it
      the Lord's wrath
      rattling tares loose from
      the earth's embrace.

When the midwife trots in
along the bow of the river,

she sees wrists and ankles
swollen purple
and rash-pimpled skin

splitting at the crevices
like rotten melon rind.

The white
behind the mother's green eye
softly mottled
blood-shot capillaries
      like a rooster's marked egg—

          brain quaking
          in its shale-brittle skullcap.

So she leaves off
her homespun
conceits of mercy.

No opened scissors
are snugged
under the rope webbing
of the blankets

to cut the pain,
nor swallow's
dirt-daubed tea funneled
       into the mother's mouth.

She commends the pair of them
to providence—

assuring the woman
she will be delivered
of a child
or to her reward
       by moonrise.

The older brothers
are shuttled out to the corncrib
to wait in silence
as the earth opens,
       the Mississippi
       changes its course
       and the baby is born
       to the cramped cradle—

            34°10′43″N 82°22′45″W.

Sixth and last
of a rattling line,
his mama rasps
a name five times overridden
       and finally earned
       but soon eclipsed

when the baby's brothers peek
at his face through the blanket fold.

The oldest and cleverest
pronounces him Crescent—

      flag's heraldry for the youngest son.

Bound tight
upon the slim scythe
of rich land puckered
      between the Salundy and Corn Creek.

The baby's waxen,
fat-banded arms

already bent
on worrying the muslin free.

# CLAWS IN THE WATER

*Lazarus, b. 1826*

Born to the scattered confederacy—
       40°34′33″N 84°11′34″W.

*Wapakoneta*: white bones
      in the Shawnee tongue.

Across the boards of the cabin,
his mother
cries for the sound
      of moving water.

Her youngest sister
pours water

from one jug to another
beside her ear,

then into her mouth
with sweating hands.

First birth
pain so urgent

it longs for a current
to fix itself to.

Winter child bound
in the harvest's last floss
of soft rabbit fur.

His mama's milk
is thin and reedy
      sparse as December sun.

An uncle holds him
in the doorway of the cabin,

sweeping aside
the burst of snow
with his free hand
and waiting for the infant's
slate eyes to sliver in the light.

At four months,
the baby sucks corn porridge
from the corner of a calico rag
and teethes
across a blanched knuckle of bone.

Twelfth infant
of the year.

Quakers in thrall
to the alphabet's
exacting symmetry

baptize him Lazarus.

But that is not
        the name he turns to.

# FIRST RANGES

Herd animals' behavior
before migration curves

sound waves as river polarity beads
to the drag of different boats:

keel boat, steam ship, canoe.
Branches bound in gut and wrapped

in oiled buffalo skin, buoyantly precarious.
Trilobite resting in a child's soft palm.

*American Arithmetic*; gone ranging.
The surveyor's bright glint

of pick and chisel—*being a System
of Decimal Arithmetic made easie.*

# MAPSICK

*Geodaesia: The Art of Surveying and Measuring of Land Made Easie* by John Love is a canonical treatise on surveying. The book was first issued in 1688 and was widely used in the early colonial surveying of America. Copies of the text were willed to oldest sons and kept on high shelves far from apprentices. They traveled west wrapped in calico and nestled in saddlebags. Small enough to palm, the text was paper alchemy: a magnet pulling lines up to the surface of the land it swept over.

From contact, European colonizers brought a radically different worldview regarding possession and ownership of land that was in violent opposition to that of the Indigenous Americans. It is a vast oversimplification to state that all Indigenous people simply held the land in common. Native people had varied, sophisticated, and sometimes contentious systems of living on and claiming their land, but the colonial impulse to survey, measure, and possess territory was deeply foreign.

Descended from both the colonizers and the Indigenous people of America, my lineage drafts the mathematical record of meridians and baselines in a cryptic code that encapsulates the bloody history of this continent. When I look at a map, a toxic prickle of infirmity ripples through me. It is like the uncanny shift in the mirror when I see the shadow of my exuberant body moving in smooth health undulating into the disaggregated systems of illness. I map myself into frozen joints, weak blood, and lacy bones; these measurements slip into a web over my frontiers.

# FRONTIER ARITHMETIC

During supper,
as his father begs
the Lord's forgiveness
for his failure
as an earth tiller,

Crescent's stubby finger
tallies of its own accord—
       sums on the slab
       of his kneecap.

The grandfather raves over his bowl
       demanding a lost medal from
       the Chickamauga Wars.

The boy puzzles
frontier arithmetic:
stone fruit small and miserly
left to rot into the ground,
bites of gristle
on the rough slate of his plate,
bolts of calico, twists of cornmeal,
envelopes of Rio coffee
       so fine they are stored
       in the corners
       of his mama's trousseau.

Days remaining.

Crescent tugs a smile
from the trail guide's
silent woman
       with his whispered word, *auntie*.

Later, his grandfather's pronged grip
on his elbow
as he hauls the boy
onto the back of the woman's saddle roll.
            *Don't call that woman anything.*
                    *She's no kin to you.*

A child's salute:
each stout finger
and his two blunt thumbs
drumming along the horse's haunches,

ten soft thuds
for the last words
            he ever hears
            from the man.

On the trail
the woman teaches
him phrases in Cherokee
for the quality of the earth
near the river's fork,
and the misting horizon line
            of stacked mountains
                    rippling into the distance.

She passes him a Shawnee cake
wrapped around a nob of bacon grease

then bids him swallow it
and the words quickly

before any of the others
look back.
A week later
she peels away
            along a stream bank
            into the funnel of the Cumberland Gap.

Crescent is on foot
for the remainder

watching the dull flank
of his brother's dun mare

and balancing a bolt
of nut-brown homespun
        across the miles of water and moss.

# OBLIGATE

Passing through canebrakes
in the whelping season;
dull echo of beaver tails thudding
  through the insect swarm.

Lazarus wears
a leaden shroud
across his spine—
  his removal road year.

Bone plate growth
jarred by endless movement—
his walk has changed
weeded by the terrain of new paths
  so too his mind's rough
   rooted channels.

A seething greenwood fire
lures his uncle
into a Kaw camp
where he joins
a trapping party
bound north to the lakes

where beaver are still
so thick
a man can club them
dead from a standstill.

Looping a bandolier
around Lazarus' shoulders,

he makes him repeat the words
*Cape Girardeau*

37°18′33″N 89°32′47″W.
A guarantee to meet again.

Lazarus sweats
into the calico and leather
braced around his joints.

His teeth
grow loose in his gums
constantly worried
by his tongue.

He plummets
into quietness,
neck stiffening
as he stops
looking back.

Worn yellow doeskin
peeks through
the bright pointed prints
of falling leaves
beaded to the front
of the bandolier.

The warp and weave of the thread
peek sallow
through the beadwork's slow unstitching
like bleached ribs of buffalo
cleanly punctuating waves
of prairie rye.

At the end of the convoy,
Lazarus hoists his sister
onto a colt's jutting withers
making its wisp of tail
switch frantically.

He shows her how to bite
into the bald patches
of the bandolier
suck the whisper of meat
from the dry skin.

The sharp dents
of her milk teeth
            fall into line
                        with the indentations
                        of lost beads.

# LEVIATHAN

In Westport the small French cart
of the voyageurs earned the name mule-killer.

Once Shawnee was the lingua franca
up and down the Mississippi,

then *mollassi became molasses*.
For the bringing of the horse

it is said much can be forgiven: burn
of Missouri whiskey and aching molars,

lunatic fevers of cholera,
even those men

born astride. Rare beast to share
that weight on such fine and slender legs.

# LONG HUNT

Watauga River Camp
near Sycamore Shoals—

the revival preacher's railing
for crosses into the west
bores into father-ear.

      The frontier's flirting terminus
      girdles the man
      like the marks
      of a new township
      across a stand of old growth.

He calls for a blessing
before they depart for Kentucky,

names the boys
arrows in his quiver

promises them all
a place where men
stand thin and lordly
      on the velvet skin
      of the land.

The whole family
swallowed like rotgut

swirling in the mouth
of the Wilderness Trail.

Each sweating mile—
a load of nails and coffee

calico bolts and rosewater jingling
in the saddle bags measuring

      distances between
      settlements and revival camps.

His mama's quaking fear
seeps into the wagon.

Clutched woodcut illustrations
of Indian depredations
      make her swaddle
      her youngest child
      into the back corner of the wagon
      through the roughest passes.

A woman tallying love
for her children—
last to leave her body
most dearly,
but no violence
save hunger
guts the wagon train.

Crescent slips the seam
easy as a swallow's nest
knocked to earth.

He stretches his legs,
westering on the trail
and calls it in a whisper

*Athwominie*, the young down
of his tongue
nibbling away
      at the Cherokee syllables.

By summer, they have traced
revival paths
all along the Kentucky River.

At Boonesborough,
Crescent escapes
from the merchant tent
to the horse lot.

Men pay him
in swigs of whiskey
and sticky nubs
of boiled candy
to hold the leads
of their fractious horses.
       Call and reply
       of the sinners
       echoes out to them.

     *And what come ye out*
          *into the wilderness to see?*

Across the fields,
grown men prostrate themselves
in fits of religious fervor.

Prone across the wilted prairie grass,
they are so small
from the boy's vantage
like switched children hollering
their agony out
over the lilting grass tops.

     *Thy sins are all forgiven thee.*

Crescent shatters
the hard confections
against his molars,
     flicks a horsefly from his shoulder.

# TREMORS

Enraged at settler atrocities and encroachments, Tecumseh stamped his foot into the ground, trampling out the fault lines of the New Madrid earthquake. Half the nation rattled to the percussions of his dismay. The very meanders of the rivers changed. Long blades were shearing Shawnee land to the bone; sharpened nibs dripping ink were negotiating these phantom obliterations on map vellum.

The loam that applauded Tecumseh's confederacy of resistance with such might grew still with the next generation's forced removal. Even now, there are traces of the sorrow that blasted the trees into crippled crescents, warping them back into the soil along the margins of those paths of exile.

Perched on the shoulders of generational trauma sit these two theses: suffering begets cruelty begets suffering begets cruelty, and pain is empathy's catalyst. When deep hurt sears, my fists and abdomen sickle inward. I compress my atoms in a futile attempt to minimize the target. When it abates, the curve of the earth returns discernably under my soles and my fingers unclench, probing and pinching the air for the velvet current of any homeward trail.

# FORDING

Distances vast;
buffalo fewer
      antelope thunderous.

In the wake
of spring floods,
Lazarus rides the breadth

of his flat new territory
on a narrow-flanked sorrel.

He works with his uncle
to ferry wagons
of hogs and cattle
across the river.

A virgin crop
of green corn opens
to the south shore's embankment.

Lazarus shies a lariat
around a young calf's front legs,

drags the squealing parallel line
of the animal's hooves
      through the mud
      and into the water.

      At his uncle's nod from the opposite shore,
      Lazarus slips off the swimming horse,

slogs a cow
by the forelock from the current
and onto the slender bluff.

The men laugh
as he stands

one foot raised like a stork,
his instep holding a flap of skin
torn loose by a stray hoof.

Riding home
Lazarus loses himself

in a herd of spring-famished
antelope, rides in and out
of clotted sunspots

then maneuvers through two
quicksandy creeks
            to get north
            from the Sac and Fox agency.

            He ties the flap of skin on his shin
            with a braid of prairie grass,

            softly clubs his bare heels
            against the dense shed of the
                        gelding's winter coat.

# CORRECTION LINES

Crosshatching on a map
hints at depth and damage:

old quarter lines settle
into fresh furrows.

Paper trail of the stratified
renegotiation of the western frontier.

Hands that span belly to thigh return
unwillingly to the labor of the field

when the only balm to be found
is inside the rip between skin and meat.

How hard to hold a stick in the hand
without swinging it.

Inside the man, survey the boy
with horse oats in his mouth,

shadow of the branch blooming
in blood across his shoulders.

# AUCTION OF THE BONDED

Perched on Kentucky's
ragged edge,
Crescent's grown handsome: dark hair,
spit-bug-green eyes, an ache

in wrist and eyeteeth
no axe swinging can slake.

Sowing a taste for leaving,
the whistling hiss
of his scythe severing

his father's sparse crop
turns him inside out.

      A pocket that aches
      to be filled.

Calico and honey
sell slow on the frontier—

sixteenth harvest skin,
not his own

but a waltz partner
jerking him roughly
      across the boards.

Father and older brothers
turn their minds

to a new trade,
cash bounties,
back room scalps,
panthers and wolves.

After November's auction
of the indentured poor,

Crescent signs papers
with a surveyor
      up the National Road.

On the river ride home,
he fixes his eyes high—
palisades of bird's-eye limestone
      stacked like dusty bolts
      of hazelnut homespun on a shelf.

He walks off
wearing new boots
      for the first time in his life,
      shocked at their chafing straightness.

Strange to bend
a hard thing
with his body's will
and not the other way around;

they wear his flesh
to blood and pus
      before he's crossed into Ohio
      just the same.

# ALLOTMENT LINE

Settlers spill
in parallel currents
at the opening
of the Oregon Trail—
       knife plunged
       into a sack of grain;

their oxen lumber west
as he rides east.

At the mission,
the Delaware wait
       on the Delaware.

The Shawnee stand
on the frosted lawn

parceled—zenith sectors
of clan and age.

Lazarus crouches
at the edges,
an ant trail of indentations
press into his palm.

       Sister's wobbly stitches
       on the money handkerchief.

Heat from a horse's long susurrus of piss
melts into a puddle beneath his feet.

Inside the council house
frost eddies
in waterfalls
crevasses where

the logs are chinked
not daubed,
corners rounded with ice.

The agent allots
to each head of house.

Lazarus finds
his family is
debited for a ploughshare.
   The wrap of money lightens.

Homeward, Lazarus passes two children
dragging a travois of buffalo bones.

The girl covers her hands
with an apron
and hefts the rope;
   the boy scans the ridges
   bare palms opened
   by the frigid cord.

Women along the path
roam for the season's last plants
as the land
freezes up around them.

Faces creased
at the fingertip strangeness
of new flora.

Their bodies
still pluck
for the roots, flowers, shoots
young muscles remember,

but they are so far from home
like a tongue
poking around

in the shrill vacancy
of a shattered tooth,

groping out into the grasses
of the western land,
        unsure and unsettled.

            The aches chase the fevers.

# PAST TENSE

The last Shawnee speaker in my family was my great-grandfather. Shipped away to boarding school as a young child, his language slipped from story to sentence, sentence to fragment, fragment to adjective, leaving him with the sparsest scattering of nouns to pass down—a starvation harvest of syntax-starved images.

I know the words for elk and water. There are other Shawnee nouns as dense as koans with metaphor and meaning, but they remain inscrutable to me.

Following the Indian Removal Act of 1830, the Shawnee were forcibly evicted from their homelands to Indian Territory. In most cases, the removal took more than eighteen months. Primary source documents and the rare testimonials spared by history attest to the untenable conditions. Many Shawnee died on the removal road, particularly the society's most fragile members: the young, elderly, and ill. Upon arrival many more died due to disease, inadequate food and shelter, and violence.

I have an ancestor who, in the aftermath of the Civil War's upheavals, made an appeal to Congress in support of the Shawnee tribe. I am told he was articulate, intelligent, and literate in Shawnee, English, and Latin. He was sent to Washington to advocate for the tribe in a famine winter. He spent months there, a dark shadow in the elegant Shawnee turban and clothes of his time, relegated to the chilly corners of the antechambers of antechambers.

A man of his generation would have been removed from Ohio alongside his parents and siblings in his boyhood. He would have been removed again with his own grandchildren. By the end of his life, he would have seen his nation reduced to a tenth.

Family legend claims that he waited in the capital for a season and a half, but was met with no audience.

# METES AND BOUNDS

Chilled thigh under homespun,
the weaver's aching back

and yellowed finger pads,
quotidian aches bow to the sovereignty

of metes and bounds.
The length of cotton

stretched between brass tacks
weaves its own

ledger-worthy autonomy.
Proceed from the blazed line

twenty chains to the southwest.
Dull needle through burlap.

Chilled holler of the axe's
subtle swipe

through a scrimshaw of frost.
Under moss, an oak trunk is blazed

breast high and skin smooth
to mark the end place.

# AXE MAN

Along the terminus
of Boone's Lick Trail,

leading a mule
by a rat-tooth embossed
leather strap
figure eight wrapped
into his palm,

Crescent's boots
clunk against his neck
to spare the scuff.

Left hand stuffed
in a pocket
out of long habit
thrumming the sums—
      ochre boulders
      specked with lichen,

      light between branches,

      shadows cast over the trail
      in the space
      of one creek crossing
      to the next.

Seven months an axe man,
he cuts the juvenile trunks
of oak, maple, riparian sycamore

along the perimeters
of survey clearings

stacks them in parallel lines
of rot; vista lines
        for the true surveyor

who calls this labor
civilization's frenzied sketching
        across the vellum mapskin
        of the wilderness—
        38°57′54″N 92°44′30″W.

At the camp,
the old men
scare him with tales
of runaways,

subtle blades
in copper fists.

Portaging
through swampland
thick with disease
he's nearly gnawed clean—
canvas and skin
laid bare.

He learns
to dodge and claim,
takes in small sums

stretching the last of the beaver pelts
on withes made of hickory.

One of every dozen
blasts back at him,
        tracing its own shadow
        in blood across his torso.

Glint prisms shine
off the instruments rattling
from the saddle's tie-downs

illuminating the slim tally
            of what he owns;

one blade
that slides most readily
into his palm

slyly marked
with a waxing moon
of pooled sepia
on the bone-handle.

Kentucky slavers
follow the trampled path
of survey chains;
blast the open land
            with a stubble of slim
            shallow graves.

        Tobacco and hemp.

# GREENWOOD SMOKE

Never the same smoke
settling around his shoulders—

      Lazarus reaches high
      as he will ever grow.

Indigo ink dries
on the vellum
of preemption laws
drafted in the capital.

To the west,
flashes of movement
inside a shaded dapple
on the horizon;
fires from a camp of squatters
      blazing out as they
      move on.

To the south, a surveyor
crosses the river
      once called simply
      after the shape of its bend,
      soon to be baptized anew
      with an Irish assessor's surname.

To the east, a railroad man
sketches rigs onto a slate
      and offers bribes:
      sugar wrapped in linen,
      wan, embryonic
      coffee beans to roast.
      He rests a sodden
      gabardine overcoat
      near the fire,

waves railroad bonds
and proclaims
that the men will be made
        into Shawnee kings—

        if they will only cast their
        lots his way.

Lazarus burns
the man's paper.

Rides on
to his uncle's allotment—
        rattlesnake redolent.

The sweat rolling off him
smells like hickory,

the only water
willingly ceded
since childhood.

Until he hits
the farthest rig
and lays foundation stones,
        his only marks
        are the tracks he leaves.

# TIMBER SCRIBE

Between the membrane of fur
and muscle, blades fevered by appetite

dimpled the prairie with denuded bison.
The pick's sharp interruption

of the ground's moss and prairie grass union
uncoupled Kansas soil.

A timber scribe,
small enough to hide

in the curve of the palm;
portable instrument

of the Great Reconnaissance,
subtle gouge for the lonely mind.

# RED BRUSH SURVEYOR

On a survey
of the Platte
and Missouri Rivers,

willow branch
and buffalo hide keelboats,

braced tight and larded,
      waltz the rough current's
      white hell
      that topples a flatboat.

      Snagged and sunk
      the year's profit of furs
      flail into the water.

Crescent watches
the men kicking
their youngest apprentices
      into the waves.

He wades thigh deep
to pull a boy
up and out of the ebb.

Half drowned and grim-swaddled
in a waterlogged fur,

the child nearly drags him down
into the river.

He digs his heels
into the sand bed

jerks and hauls
until the boy is
born again riparian
          from the robe of slick fur.

The men drag the drenched pelt
up the trampled bank
as the boy sputters and quakes.
Anxious to turn his heels
on this scene,

Crescent drops his papers
at the quartermaster's shack

and rides out early,
cutting north and east.

Bluestem grass and wild rye
give way

to the girdled stands of trees
          marking a new township.

Rigs of land
broken in by settlers
rattle past like wooden dominos;
          middle children
          ever raking away
          at dirt lawns
          pause in their labor to wave.

In his last bonded year,
the frontier moves
at forty miles an earth spin.

Crescent marks his future striding
beholden to his papers still,

but with the river damp
steaming off his shoulders

and the very tools
for measuring
the skin of the earth
          in his saddlebags.

# FIRST BORN

Salt-lick deer

      split-hung
      over the saddle's pommel.

Blood fused rain-soak
runs down in rivulets
      to the gray mare's
      muddy fetlocks.

Game is scarce
but the long ride
shakes more flavor
into the hanging meat,
      already savory
      from within.

Lazarus rides low
through prairie fringes
of post oak and blackjack.
      Frail sun
      dries his mare's
      coat into pink-larded waves.

Wisps of stone fruit scions
loll in the back rig
of the oozing meadow.

Rich, feathery belts of timber
snake lavender in dusky light
      through the buttery bottomland.

He rides close enough
to see his son,
head resting

on his wife's chest
tracery of the baby's slim veins

and dark wisps of hair
feathering across the bib
of her faded calico dress.

The deer's hooves tick across
the tip of the saddle horn
        as Lazarus dismounts
        and heaves it down.

# LAND COLIC

Indian apple leaves a remarkable down
on the prairie, so unlike anything

from the Volga grasslands to
the basalt columns hemming Ireland,

that all similes are rendered null and void.
A buffalo needs two shots

through the lungs to be brought down.
Surveyor's staccato cry

caught in a wave pressed into igneous slab:
the earth's colicky sobs.

Northwest running meridians
and east–west base lines

embossed with corner markers
destined to be lost

or obliterated if not chiseled deep
into the vernacular rock.

# TERRITORIAL THIRST

Peaked pommel
round the front of his hips—

his vertebrae
dance and crackle

in a dysentery waltz.
Rigs fan in his wake—
      a jumping-off trail
      from Saint Louis.

Lately shrugged
of his bond papers;
      dirty bandage peeled
      from suppurating wound.

The saddle's leather croak
splinters in his left ear—
      tender throb and relief
      cups his jaw in equal measure.

His eyes are fever cataracts,
but keen
      subtle angles

small machines of measurement
jangle at his thighs.

Evidence of the first task
of the frontier—
to break down the grasses

make a dirt lawn,
then start killing the snakes.

Indian Territory's lofty bluestem grass
embroiders compacted prairie.

Listing shacks and irregular
farm patches

warble along the margins
of the path
where the corn
balks at the hard earth
of this new country

then sinks in and sighs,
flourishing in the new-broken lushness.

When he fords
the south fork of a listless river,
his mare flicks yellow clay
from her pastern
with an irritated efficiency

knocking a languid whiff of decay
from the break

and he remembers
lean years
sucking the horses' cracked oats
for the hint of molasses,
        how the smell of
        dried flakes of timothy
        was almost food.

He thanks all creation
for nothing
but the vantage
she affords.

Bloated and thirsting,
he knows he must noon
under shade and wait out the sun,

yet to ride on or stop
            will surely kill him.

Dipping his hand
into a slow stream,
            tadpoles ripple between his fingers.

He lurches
into a border trading post

where the trader's wife
feeds him bread burned black
for worms and doses him with tonic.

She bids him
to keep a lynx eye
on the small Indian boy
sweeping out the shop.

            Old signs for bounty scalps yellow
            next to newer signs
            for slave auctions;

            brass tacked and greased with wear
            they flutter over him
            as he drowses in a corner.

# COMPROMISED

As with nations, so too within the individual body, the concept of lines and borders is fraught. American history once established a mathematical line that arbitrarily freed or enslaved the human body as it crossed it. When I write the numbers of the Missouri Compromise, I can't question the atrocities that a nation capable of such thinking could commit, but I wonder what form of cruelty it could possibly consider excessive.

American history compels me to imagine my own body quartered. I see the paper that measures the quantum of my Shawnee blood. I become troubled and wonder what nation is it that claims my pen hand as I impose these words on the page.

# EATING THE TURTLE

Favored men
grow thick,
tonguing smooth brine,

buttered meat,
        stone-fruit sweet.

Bodies soften,
appendages evolve—
hands grow hooked

around split rail fences,
flatten and spatulate
over quill-curve.

Treaty papers
pull moisture
from the whorls
        of index fingers.

Resistance deep
into the south
along the marsh river
thick with swans,
        38°36′43″N 95°15′59″W
        —Starved Rock.

Little girls kneel
in the canebrakes,
gigging for small fish and frogs
at the ends of rusted nails.

Men stand hunched,
faces large on attenuated bodies

as they pull an ancient turtle
from the river
once called Grasshopper,
            now named Delaware.

They rip into its underside
with picks and cook

a slow stew
            in the animal's shell.

# CHAINS AND LINKS

*I do desire*—Chillicothe, Piqua, Lima
*that you remain*—Shawnee, Lawrence, Olathe

Wyandotte, Tecumseh—*on the other side*
Junction City, Fort Leavenworth, Lenexa—

*of the river.* Species shame goes to earth
at the piedmont. 1844's flooding of the Kaw:

long rains chased by dry and hot weather,
coupled with the smallpox, cholera, and typhus

trailed by settlers. Buckskins, bucks
becoming frontier currency.

At the fall line where ships unload and lighten,
fever, chills, bloody flux. Let the record state

in that year, *that there was not
a single well person in that nation.*

# MISSISSIPPI PANORAMA

Grunts of the crew
cordelling upriver

soften through a sandbar.
Sparse lights
clot thicker

in the southway flow
where a floating greenhouse
of exotic plants

slips between sleeper trees
       and billows
       a sleek hum
       of chartreuse rot.

Crescent's survey crew pauses
at a bonfire rendezvous

nestled inside a horseshoe bend
south of
       36°35′16″N 89°32′9″W.

They drink
a newspaper man's proffered anisette

and listen to his lament
for copy.

His panorama painter
nods at an assistant

to unload slender
glass flasks of linseed oil.

These strangers start wary
        spooked by rumors
        of Yellow Jack
        moving down the riverbank,
        but the drinks soothe their reserve.

Loquacious and loose,
one man allows

that you can buy inoculations
off the Indian Agents

on the other side of the river
that buffer the disease,

though he doesn't trust such things
        and wouldn't truly credit
        the rumor enough
        to merit the crossing.

The newspaper man confesses
to all who will listen

that he's bent
on fabricating
a story of gruesome atrocity
        in the west—a thicket of corpses
        to sell to the eastern papers.

The next morning,
they move to the marrow-searing
flask of rye.

The painter
stretches his canvas on a knoll.

Soul drivers unlash
their flatboats
from the floating cities,

shrugging their vigilance
as they round the Kentucky Bend
        into the heel of Missouri.

They step to land,
anxious to trade for gulps
of honey brandy
to chase off the milk-sick fly.
        They bring a girl.

By the flat-blue hour,
the painter is dead drunk
        raving at them

to drag her out
of his sightline.

He flicks paint
across cinnamon roots
as he lurches,

digs a filthy fingernail
in frustration
across the bottom of the wet canvas.

As Crescent pulls her away,
a thicket of straw
stuffed behind her head
scatters into a quicksilver corona.

He misjudges her lightness
grip slithering around her ankle:

her heel is calloused,
but each toe

still holds a child's plump
curves and neat nails,

smooth and tidy
as walleye scales.

Her clothes are stained,
she smells like metal;
rusty plumes of bog tannin
      leech into the river
      in patches
      all around them.

A preacher tree
bobs up and down
into the water

baptized in loose silt
      of Mississippi relish.

# THE COMING MEN

Harvest's slender punctuation—

metal posts
buried deep and braced
            with wood frames.
Washington's winter dreams
are laid down

intercontinentally.
Rigs and parallel lines

        of railroad tracks—

        gloaming verges.

Fresh ligatures
of telegraph wires unspooling.

Opposition—
soft fall
of pale
stone-fruit

blossoms unfurling
loosely on the land.

Dig out
the granite corner markers
capped in numbered brass,

blaze random
marks in the haggard
stands of hardwoods.

Public auction and preemption
scatters two million
Delaware and Shawnee acres.

The frontier's jittering threshold
shuttles along the mapskin.

Squatters take the orchard land.

1856 brings forth a winter
so bitterly cold—

      deerskins hanging in the trees freeze hard.

      All signs for an auspicious
      planting failing
      in cold, dry weather
      and marshy prairie.

Lazarus holds his fistful
of broken nails
and obliterated

government corner markers
in one hand,
a troublemaker's allotment
in the other.

His daughter wears new brass earrings;
      etched numbers bracketing her round face.

The only velvet warmth
to be found

in the territory
is in the crook
of a horse's mouth
      at the bottom of the bit.

# PAIN SCALE TREATIES

Historians surmise that at a peak in westward expansion, the 1830s through the 1840s, the frontier of European settlement moved at a rate of ten to forty miles a year. I used to wince at photocopies of old treaty papers—fragile shrouds from this voracious consumption.

The Shawnee, like so many of America's sovereign Indigenous nations, signed many treaties with the colonial and American government:
1786's Treaty with the Shawnee conducted at the mouth of the Great Miami River;
1795's Treaty of Greeneville;
1803's Treaty of Fort Wayne;
1805's Treaty with the Wyandotte held at Fort Industry;
1808's Treaty with the Chippewa conducted at Brownstown;
1814, 1815, 1817, and 1818's Treaties with the Wyandotte;
1825's Treaty with the Shawnee conducted in St. Louis;
1831's Treaty with the Shawnee concluded at Wapaghkonnetta;
1831's Treaty with the Seneca in Logan Country, Ohio;
1832's Treaty with the Shawnee;
1832's Treaty with the Shawnee made at Castor Hill in Missouri;
1832's Treaty with the Seneca and Shawnee concluded at the Seneca agency, on the headwaters of the Cowskin River;
1854's Treaty with the Shawnee made in the city of Washington;
1865's Agreement with The Cherokee and Other Tribes in The Indian Territory;
1867's Treaty with the Seneca, Mixed Seneca and Shawnee, Quapaw, Etc.

The gore of the battlefield seeps into the ground and is lost; ink on vellum is its approximation.

I am laid low on a bed of dried blood, but it has been graciously consumed by the hospital's large, absorbent sheet guards and rendered into rusty shadows under the paper's tender layers.

Any treaty is an artifact of unimaginable suffering.

Only twice do I attempt to articulate my discomfort in my own terms, once in a sham attempt at restrained stoicism, I say that it is hitting a raw nerve, then in hysterics, I whimper that I see the glint of the teeth and at once they are clamped down inside me. The third time I have learned to say that it is a seven and accept the quicksilver pulse of intravenous analgesic like a benediction.

I recognize that I have made a treaty with myself bartering the refinement of my language for rapidly delivered slivers of chemical mercy. My extremities talk for me now. When I hold up the numbers of the pain scale, I feel a shiver of what I have ceded with such terrified alacrity.

I sign my new mark in the air with my dominant hand.

# INSTRUMENTS OF THE
# TRUE MEASURE

Moving lines of settlement
are baptized in the bile

of their own digestion.
Chickasaw in the northern parcel of the state

Choctaw in the central.
Domesday Book scrolls meld into the

linen press
of the Kansas-Nebraska Act.

Reliance on the crude materials of measure
bows to precision. Watery ink

like corn mash bourbon haloing the mouth:
dress the shale in a trickster's uniform,

stretch marked by the moving zeniths.
The First, Second, Third, Fourth Principal Meridians.

*Thence west on a blank line*
to the Indian Meridian.

# COMPASS ROSE

The black line top
of his ledger—
      finest possession,

an elegant and even
compass man's hand

goads then steadies
inside the coarse amber cradle
      of Missouri whiskey.

Crescent moves west
tracking Kansas blood

toward the foothills
of the Rockies.

He pilfers
into the dry belly
of a parcel
fingers stroking
through a soft wrap
of maps

Flakes of octavo pages
pressed from creamy linen
give way to his probing—
      no living skin
      stays so clean.

Cairo men hustle
the marketplace and forts

selling infected blankets,
commissioning rotten supplies
   for Indian removal.

Ohio water,
known to make a man
sweat sweet,

refuses to mix
with the turbid stew
of middleway swell.

Rain funnels down
the pen tip
and muddies fresh lines
on his paper.

He sullies the edges
with a slip
of ink and grime,
the slim spool
   of his index print
   delicate as the bowl
   of a silver teaspoon.

Shaded strokes show
igneous rock

crosshatching hints
at silver deposits
on a map calling for miners.

Sudden jolt of the collapsing bluff
drives the nib

hard into his calloused palm
and infection
makes the scar a lasting keloid
   wound of measurement and avarice.

# THE DUCK'S EGG

New land again.

> New land
> gain noted
> in the creamy ripple
> of a government ledger book.

They ride south chased
by the paper swish of treaty.

A woman swirls
a pinch of meal
       into still water

cooks a limpid gruel
around the silver mounds
       of firestones in the pot.

The baby chases for a locust
with dry-eyed intent,

then sits on a tipped saddle
whining and wringing
worn stirrup leather
       against her gums.

Lazarus takes his oldest boy
to scout for food.

He watches the boy spur
his bare heels
against the pony's slight flanks,

disappearing into a buffalo wallow so deep,
he sees just the wispy tips
of sorrel forelock
   and the boy's fine dark hairs
   swaying in the movement.

With the boy out of sight
for the moment,
   Lazarus lists
   on the saddle blanket—

   a hollow throb
   under his ribs as he leans
   deep into a cramp
   with one hand clamped
     on the horse's withers.

He remembers a hunting camp
of his own childhood;

his uncle's grin
as he sauntered on his knees
before the door flap

having sunk a curious elk
clean through the lungs

with his blanket still
   sleep-wrapped across his chest.

This giant's land
is sparse and miserly.

At noon, he gazes deeply
into it, as if
   he could see his children's faces
   under the frosted crust of the horizon.

In the absence of game,
they find the haunches
of a horse's skeleton.

A wayward immigrant's
abandoned dining table
with curved oak legs
and a family crest of stags
        bleached in the prairie sun.

The boy leads
his pony with the leather
loose in one hand.

He pauses to prod
an embossed stallion
rearing across the loose slats
of a broken headboard.

Crouching at a burl
beside a near-dry stream
in the soft
opal light
        of near dark,

Lazarus calls the boy back to him—
his voice
the father's confluence
        of irritation and sorrow.

When the child jogs carefully back,
his mouth is twisted to hide a smile,

arms tight
around a clutch
of the last of the season's duck eggs.

He rides the cache
back to the camp
cradled in his lap
in a basket of rank weed.

Around the fire,
they dust ash
from the cooked eggs.

The baby gags on one,
too far along

with the feathers and spine
of the developing bird.

Lazarus holds her mouth
shut around it
as she struggles

until he feels the soft click
of her new teeth

around the gestational bones
and the lump of meat
            shudders down her throat.

# BLAZED TRUNK

Devoid of new frontiers
since the Romans mortared Hadrian's Wall,

settlers' ancestors saw the axe's blazed union
in the milk wood of the living tree

as a horse's lean face.
Nautilus spiral, township squares:

newly ratified treaties diminish the land
with mathematical exactitude,

each acre to be paid out in trust.
As the rigs curve

smaller and smaller
in a Fibonacci sequence,

the walking body is fractioned—
possession following measurement.

Numerated agony made linear
as with the bondage line of 36°30´.

# THE LAND CROW

Soft pleasure wrap
of coins enveloped in bills

rests near his thigh.
His free hand
drums over the warp of fabric
across his knee.

As compass man,
he can hold no weapon—

metal splays the magnets
too erratically.

A hired gunman rides
the perimeter. Searching
the rain crow—
        all signs skittish in dry weather.

Settlers follow the surveyors
furtively as a mud-soaked hem—
        sibilant swish of riders.

A boy in the camp
minds the hogs
and rubs a young sow's milk
into his eyelids
to try and read the wind.

Crescent feels a gnaw
when he sees the boy,

fatherless, ragged ribs heaving
under an axe swing

or ranging on foot
for scraps of firewood.

There is a shrunken apple
that rolls in Crescent's saddlebag
and he wishes
he could lob it to the boy.

He eats it
to kill the impulse,
a grainy pudding of crabbed rot
under the taut red skin.

Rough hued log cabins
dimple the edges of the territory—

what fences there are
crowned with snakes

pinioned belly up
to woo the clouds.

Crescent sketches
a cadastral survey

on the back of a call
for more settlers
from the Volga.

Old language drags
along the drunken
splay of their
broken heels:

  *Rivals* from the Latin for river.

  *Slake* for the old Anglo-Saxon for slew.

He intones
from the surveyor's manual:
     *Abandoned,*
          *forsaken entirely,*
               *vested in no one,*

encourages the squatters
to drop their foundation posts

on the far side of this river.

# ONION SKIN

Portents of fierce winter
undermined by movement:

the age-old songs
of chill warning

grow sparse
over stretched miles and
        vexing meridians.

Corn that sprouts lushly
then offers abundant ears

on the banks of the Scioto
gives way

to the thin skins
of allotment onions
along the lower banks
        of the Kaw.

A subtle conjuring
winds under the skin

when the tract
severed in twain

twangs within the body;
        new lots break
        into fractions
        alongside the nations.

Of the thousand
who walked from Ohio,

Lazarus, his wife
and their three surviving children
drop a loose square
of foundation logs—
        36°50′25″N 94°36′36″W.

A prairie wolf
at the edge of the camp

grows bold enough
to gnaw at the dried blood

that still clings
        to the saddle's rawhide ties.

Some say an onion,
halved and burned
black over hardwood

then pressed
to the torso
will lift the wet rack
        of consumption.

When the first spring breaks,
the survivors
wear a layered blister

straddling the hollow of their chests;
        green corn sprouts slender.

# THE IMMACULATE GRID

*From the red river*
*northward to 36° 30´ and thence westward*

*stick* then *stuck.* What feature
trapped the surveyor's greeting call?

Bars, basins, falls, flats
gaps, guts, ranges, rapids,

springs, swamps, summits.
Intersection of the Indian Meridian

and the Indian Base Line.
Arrowheads articulated

by size and point
count slick coup

on museum walls.
The word for the pin

that held the surveyor's chain
in place was arrow.

# PARTING CALL

A timber scribe is a small, sharp gouge designed for blazing trees. This tool, trim enough to fit in a pocket, was once the first and most essential component of any surveyor's gear.

*Stick* as anachronism; the traditional bellow of the surveyor as the blaze is carved into the sight-trunk and the first chain is placed.

*Stick*: seven marks are carved into my torso and abdomen. I meander into the territory of illness and must learn to make its land my own; my body's sovereignty evaporates.

Is it mercy or cruelty that obliges the surgeon to sign her initials on the layer of skin above the first incision so that, as her scalpel begins to perforate my flesh, she is compelled to cut through her own name? A narrow conduit is surgically buried deep in my body—a portal that obliterates my skin's compromised frontiers.

The myth of the America landmass as virgin soil is pervasive. I don't see my former self as pure, but something integral is stripped from me just the same as I disaggregate into the numbers of disease. I am no longer a mystery. No dark stand of untouched timber is left in me. The exact equations of my survival are tallied—hourly, daily, weekly, monthly; mathematically.

I have one ancestor who surveyed in the American south just after the period of removal. I have another, Shawnee, a voice from Indian Territory: *I don't like those lines running so close to what's mine.*

*Stuck*: the response to the surveyor's call and the confirmation of the act of measurement.

# ABOUT THE AUTHOR

**Laura Da'** is a poet and a public school teacher. A lifetime resident of the Pacific Northwest, Da' studied creative writing at the University of Washington and the Institute of American Indian Arts. She is Eastern Shawnee. Da' is a recipient of a 2015 Native Arts and Cultures Foundation Fellowship. Her first chapbook, *The Tecumseh Motel*, was published in *Effigies II*. In 2015, Da' was both a Made at Hugo House Fellow and a Jack Straw Fellow. *Tributaries*, Da's first book, was published by the University of Arizona Press and won a 2016 American Book Award.